MARKETING BOOKS TO AUSTRALIAN LIBRARIES

GET YOUR BOOKS INTO AUSTRALIAN LIBRARIES, SELL MORE BOOKS, EARN MORE ROYALTIES

EBONY MCKENNA

This edition Copyright © 2021 Ebony McKenna

ebook ISBN 978-1-540176-09-7

print ISBN 978-1-922486-13-4

First published 2018, as *Get Your Book Into Australian Libraries*

For librarians

GET READY TO MARKET YOUR BOOKS TO LIBRARIES

Congratulations on your purchase of *Marketing Books To Australian Libraries* - or borrowing it, if you've borrowed this from a library!

As this is a print book, the links won't work. (I've tried, but my fingers don't have wi-fi). The easy solution is to go to my website

www.ebonymckenna.com

Where there's a page of updated links, which I can keep updating for years to come.

This book will help authors sell more books and earn more royalties.

Mostly, it will be for printed books - paperbacks and hardcovers. But it is also relevant for ebooks and audio. Libraries are physically closed during Covid lockdowns, but ebook and audio lending carries on, which is wonderful.

This book began life as a month-long workshop with the Romance Writers of Australia. I am a long-standing RWA member and wanted to share what I knew about the process (having done it many times myself) with my fellow writers.

Here is the basic workflow that we're going to work through:

1. **Buy Australian ISBNs** from Thorpe Bowker / myidentifiers.com.au
2. **Assign an ISBN** to each of your book titles in each format.
3. **Publish your ebook/audiobook** to the world if you're publishing electronically.
4. **Publish your print book** to the world if you're going into print, which I highly recommend. This will involve several stages of choosing a printer and selecting distribution. Ingram Spark are my personal favourite, and they now list major library suppliers amongst their distribution channels, meaning the suppliers can order directly from the printer, saving you time and money.
5. **Work out your pricing**, especially for print editions. **Pricing includes:**
6. **#POSTAGE COSTS – where you might lose money up front to get your books into libraries, but you'll make it back with PLR and then some.**
7. **#DISCOUNTS for library suppliers (some of them want such deep discounts you'll wonder if it's worth it.)**

8. **Contact library suppliers** around Australia – I'll provide a list for you to contact individually, as professionally as possible. This will involve filling out multiple forms and you will go cross-eyed. Or maybe that's just me. (But also, if you've put all your details into your 'myidentifyers' page on Thorpe Bowker, you can copy and paste instead of writing it out every time.)

9. **Make 'sell sheets'** which you can email out to libraries.

10. **Contact the actual libraries** themselves to let them know your books are with the library suppliers, and send them your sell sheets. (See how far down this is on the list? It's basically your second last stage. That's why you don't just print your books and take them in yourself.)

11. **Lending Rights** – step-by-step instructions for how to fill out the forms and get royalties every year for your printed books! Yes, our taxes at work!

That's a lot to get through! Luckily, I've broken tasks into manageable chunks so we can check things off as we go.

WHO IS THIS?

Ah yes, my credentials. I'm your host with the mos–ADHD, Ebony McKenna. I'm the author of 8 YA romance novels (in libraries across this beautiful country) heaps of Regency Novellas as Ebony Oaten and the odd contemporary, which I write as Ebony Jean. It gets crowded in here!

I'm also the author of several Self-Publishing Fundamental guides, which are mostly in ebook as the self-publishing landscape keeps changing and rebranding.

I send my print and ebooks out to libraries as I go. (I haven't made audio - yet)

In other words, I'm on this journey with you, right now.

In *other* other words, I've made plenty of mistakes and wasted loads of time. Now I've climbed out of the pits I fell into, and mapped out a more direct course, so you can learn from my mistakes.

This book will work for self-published writers as well as writers published with small presses. Traditionally published authors will also learn about the process and will be able to give their books a nudge in the right direction.

It will also work for everyone who wants to earn 'Lending Rights' with their printed books. I know authors who are published with traditional publishers who missed out on Lending Rights; the publisher assumed the author knew about them.

I discovered Lending Rights, when my Australian publisher sent their authors an email reminding us to register. This was in the publisher's interests, as publishers get Lending Rights as well. But get this - Publishers can't claim Lending Rights until the author registers for them.

Lending Rights are PLR and ELR; Public Lending Rights and Educational Lending Rights. This is a payment for the number of copies of your books on

public and school library shelves. You get the payment once a year and it really is fabulous.

Lending Rights are not available for ebooks or audio in Australia – yet. BUT readers borrow them in their thousands from libraries, so this is a great opportunity to get your books in front of readers' eyeballs.

GET THE TIMING RIGHT!

Generally, educational libraries' budgeted years run from January to December. They have money to spend on books earlier in the year. It's often the same for school libraries too. But then they also have money 'left over' in the budget, which they need to spend before the year runs out.

Public libraries in general are on a July to June financial year, like the rest of us tax-paying schlubs, which is incredibly helpful as that means lots of purchases in March and November for one lot, and many more in June and August for others.

It's all about getting your figurative ducks in a row, so that when you do contact libraries and tell them about your brilliant book/s, everything will be in place for the library to place orders without any hassles.

LEGAL DEPOSIT, NATIONAL LIBRARY OF AUSTRALIA AND HAVING A MARC RECORD

FROM THE AUGUST 2019 UPDATE

Some of my author friends were hitting a roadblock when registering for Lending Rights (which is a process I go into, in depth, later on in this book.)

They were rejected from registering because there was no 'pre-existing record' or MARC record of their book.

MARC stands for MAchine Readable Catalogue.

The Lending Rights people (beautiful, wonderful people) recommend all authors lodge their books with the NLA, the National Library of Australia. This is a good thing to do. You are a publisher now, so it's a requirement that all publishers lodge what's called a Legal Deposit (ie, send your books to them.)

This issue pops up if you're using an ISBN sourced from outside Australia (yeah, I'm talking about KDP). The 'I' in ISBN is International, it shouldn't matter, but it does.

Here's why:

When you buy your ISBN from Thorpe Bowker, the official Australian supplier, you are then registered as the owner /

publisher of those ISBNs. (You're a publisher now!) Yes, ISBNs are international, but the ones from Thorpe Bowker are Australian.

When you fill in the details of your title and ISBN, using Thorpe Bowker's myidentifiers.com register, you are creating your first **Australian** record. Once you do that, web bots and 'spiders' automatically collect that data and send it flinging all over the place, telling the world, 'This ISBN belongs to this Australian book, written by this Australian author, and here are the details.'

When you later register for Australian Lending Rights, the bots and spiders have sent out your existing Australian record. It's now Machine Readable, so will match your Lending Rights Claim to your book title and ISBN.

Then you can also send your books to the NLA, because it's a requirement.

If you've used an ISBN from another country - whether it was free or not - there will not be an existing Australian record for that book. The publisher will also be listed as whoever supplied the ISBN, not you.

You want to be the publisher, because that means more Lending Rights for you.

PART 1

DOING THINGS IN THE RIGHT ORDER, RIGHT
FROM THE START.

CHAPTER 1

SELLING MORE BOOKS, EARNING MORE ROYALTIES

IN OTHER WORDS, DOING THINGS IN THE RIGHT ORDER, RIGHT FROM THE START

THIS BOOK SHOWS the right way to approach libraries, so that you, the author (who might be right now reading this in your curry-stained pyjamas) will present yourself as a total professional at all times.

Please don't turn up to your local library with books to donate.

Why?

1. It's unprofessional
2. Did they even know you were coming?
3. Where will they catalogue the books if they didn't know you were coming?
4. Awkwards!
5. If your book does prove popular, how is the library going to order more copies in? Will they call you to donate more?

6. Donating books is not a sustainable business model.
7. This is the business side of writing, treat it as a business.

Some authors suggest asking friends to call in at their local library and request they get your book. This will only work if your book is 'in the system' and available to order. It's also asking a lot from your friends.

THIS PART'S MANAGEABLE TASKS:

It's all about getting your books 'in the system' and making your book available with official library suppliers.

- getting your ISBNs
- assigning one ISBN to each format of your book (if you're going paperback and hardback for example)
- making yourself the publisher (if you're self-publishing)
- Working out book prices **for your print runs**, whether self-published or if you're ordering in your own copies if you're published with a small press.

Writers published with small and large presses, you are definitely part of this too.

You won't need to do *quite* as much work, but you will need to create an information file for each of your titles, because you will need this information when you contact library suppliers. (Being able to copy and paste information saves so much time.)

In order to get the best out of this ebook, I recommend reading everything (or at least skimming) first, then going back and doing the work.

There is a lot to take in and it can be confusing at first.

OK then, off we go!

CHAPTER 2

ISBN AU-GO-GO

(AND DON'T STRESS ABOUT BAR CODES)

EVERY PAPERBACK WILL NEED its own ISBN (International Standard (or Standardised) Book Number) in order to:

1. Help libraries and library suppliers order the right book
2. Help Authors claim lending rights further down the track.

Even if you're only publishing ebooks at the moment, you still need to know how this works. (And then, honestly, what are you waiting for? Get into print!)

If your ebooks are already published on Kindle with an amazon ASIN (Amazon's version of the ISBN), that's fine for now, but if you want your ebooks in libraries and you want to make sure you are listed as the publisher (instead of Kindle or

Blurb or Smashwords being your publisher,) then consider buying and using your own ISBNs to make editions that are truly yours.

Being the publisher means buying ISBNs and registering them as 'yours' in your name, or a publishing name that you create. Some internet organisations will sell you 100 ISBNs for $10 - which seems amazing up front. However, after you buy them you realise the ISBNs can't have you listed as the publisher but some mob called 'ISBNFactoryThanksForYourMoney' etc. You've just blown $10, but worse than that, you've wasted your time.

Some printers and distributors offer ISBNs as well, like Kindle Direct Publishing (KDP) and IngramSpark (IS) but beware you don't lock yourself out of potential markets by doing this.

I recommend Australian authors buy their ISBNs from Thorpe Bowker (TB). TB are the official retailer of ISBNs in this country, and you will be registered as the publisher.

YOUR FIRST JOB (HOW EXCITING!)

Click on this link and follow the instructions to register with myidentifiers, so that you're ready to purchase your ISBNs.

https://www.myidentifiers.com.au

You'll see some prices on offer, and at first it might make your stomach do that hideous swooping thing.

1 ISBN for $44? That's too high.

10 ISBNs though is 'only' $88 and makes much more sense.

100 ISBNs is $480, an excellent bulk deal, and perfect for careerwriters with several books in a few formats each.

There is a one-off set-up fee which was $55 last time I checked.

BAR CODES

There's no need to buy barcodes. When you use Ingram Spark's Cover Template, you enter your ISBN in the details and IS automatically create a barcode to match your ISBN on the back.

Thorpe Bowker have special deals to get barcodes which match your ISBN, but to me it's more of a 'do you want fries with that?' up-sell.

ONCE YOU GET YOUR ISBNS, REMEMBER THIS:

You can only use each ISBN once. Once you've used it, you can't then cancel the book you've assigned it to and re-use the ISBN for a new book.

Take your time and try not to make (expensive) mistakes.

Each format of your book needs its own ISBN. For example, a paperback edition in 5x8 size, needs a different ISBN to your 6x9 'large print'. If you're making a hardback edition, you'll need an ISBN for that as well. And the ebook and an audio. That's up to five ISBNs for one title.

Ebooks only need one ISBN for distributing to to all the platforms.

HONESTY TIME:

I have ~~seven~~ eight novels out, in paperback, in libraries. (#Humblebrag) So far, I haven't really bothered with promoting the ebooks. I write Young Adult, and most teens love holding physical books. I keep hearing researchers say tablet devices make teens feel like they're doing homework.

Further down the track, when you come to register with Lending Rights, you must match your ISBNs to each paperback. Frustratingly, PLR is only for physical books at this stage and not ebooks or audio, but the Australian Society of Authors (ASA) is campaigning hard for ebook and audio Digital Lending Rights.

Has your stomach done another flip because you don't have paperbacks? That's OK. It's just as important to get your ebooks and audio into libraries – it's where the readers are, and you want readers. And I hope that as you work through this guide book, you'll see that although going into print is daunting at first, it's achievable. I mean if I can do it with my squirrel brain, then you can too.

CHAPTER 3

BECOMING YOUR OWN PUBLISHER

BECAUSE YOU'RE IN BUSINESS NOW, SO TREAT THIS AS A BUSINESS

YOU'RE BUYING your own ISBNs, which officially makes you the publisher of your books.

That means when you put your ebooks and print books out there for sale, you use the ISBN registered to you. Please remember to use your author name or your publishing house/company name.

You don't have to start a whole new company. Just use your author name. Or something. You can register a business name if you want (with the ATO) and get yourself an ABN and be in acronym heaven. Knock yourself out.

I made a dopey mistake when I put an earlier book through Ingram Spark and selected my married name as the publisher. Whoops! That's my legal name but not my author name. (Which is technically my legal name, but still.) Not a huge problem, and I've fixed it now. It's not like writing Young Adult is going to get me fired from my workplace. (Oh yeah, I work from home.) But if you work for - just spitballing here - a conservative religious organisation, or you're planning a tilt at politics, it might be a good idea to have the publisher / author name separate from the surname people know and love you for, and not something that might land you in trouble with your boss.

PUTTING YOUR BOOKS OUT THERE.

This is obviously a very important stage. I am assuming most people are fairly familiar with the process of creating ebooks and print books, whether as a print run or POD (print on demand) or putting things through Smashwords/Draft2Digital/Amazon etc.

Rather than re-invent that wheel, here's a brilliant website to check out, looking at the pros and cons of Ingram Spark and Create Space (Which is now KDP Print) for your print books.

https://selfpublishingadvice.org/watchdog-ingram-spark-vs-createspace-for-self-publishing-print-books/

(Please go to my website - www.ebonymckenna.com - all the links are there on the Self-Publishing page.)

BONUS

I have put this bonus further in the book so that people who have read this far get the benefit - rather than just people flicking through the first couple of pages.

I have not had to pay to list any of my paperbacks with Ingram Spark. (But I have ordered plenty of books, so they've made money from me, no problem!)

How did I get this freebie?

By paying attention whenever I'm on the 'checkout' page of any internet website. There's usually a section that asks for a discount coupon. But I don't have one to hand - which is OK. **All I do is open a new browser window and search 'Company name, discount coupon', then I scroll through the results.**

I try a few coupons, and see which ones work.

Every time I've found a discount coupon for Ingram Spark, it has worked and the fee has gone from US $49 to $0. That's a pretty great success rate, yeah?

This book just paid for itself and then some. You are so welcome!

For my ebooks, I'm using Vellum and Affinity Publisher software to format them, then I'm using Draft2Digital to distribute to most stores and to library platforms like Overdrive, Baker and Taylor and Bibliotheca. Bibliotheca runs Cloud Library, which is one of the big ebook services Australian libraries use.

The big one for audio is Borrow Box, which is part of Bolinda audio.

Prior to D2D I used Smashwords and it was nice and basic and pretty easy to follow. However, I struck trouble when I tried to load an anthology with multiple authors. Smashwords wouldn't list the anthology unless I listed every contributing author as a Smashwords author. It was honestly too much effort.

Even though Draft2Digital will load directly to Amazon, by

doing so they take too much of a royalty, so I load my titles directly on to Amazon. That's still where I sell most of my books.

You can also use Draft2Digital to format ebooks (and print books too if you want). The user interface is pretty to look at and also fairly intuitive. And it's free - all it costs is your time.

WARNING: The Libraries option on D2D won't show up as a distribution option unless your book price is $1.99 or above. I don't know why.

For print, I'm now using Ingram Spark. (I had previously used Blurb, but I.S. is more appealing to local bookstores who may want to order my titles in directly. Blurb are also really user friendly, and they print in the same place as Ingram Spark (in Melbourne). The quality is very good, and the binding is sturdy, which appeals to libraries.

Blurb is excellent if you have books with footnotes (cough) or want to do extra clever things with formatting.

You can use KDP (Amazon) they are now printing in Australia. This will save us a fortune on postage.

I've also heard great things about using Fuji Xerox (in Tassie) for print runs. You can do all sorts of fabulous things with the covers, so please check them out.

I'm a little wary of Lulu, because the few copies I've seen from them have that thick white paper (ideal for photos, not so great for novels). This could be down to the author's choices, I'm not sure. Also, the cost per book with Lulu gets pretty steep, whereas the copies I make from Ingram Spark are around the $8 mark for a 250 – 300 page paperback). However, Lulu will let you pick up your print order and save on postage.

Anyway, I'm going to let you investigate the best way for you to format your ebooks and print books. Google freely and read widely to learn all you can. It's a whole author guidebook in itself, really.

CHAPTER 4

ASSIGNING ISBNS TO EACH TITLE

(AND EACH FORMAT OF EACH TITLE, IF YOU HAVE HARDCOVERS AND PAPERBACKS OF THE SAME BOOK)

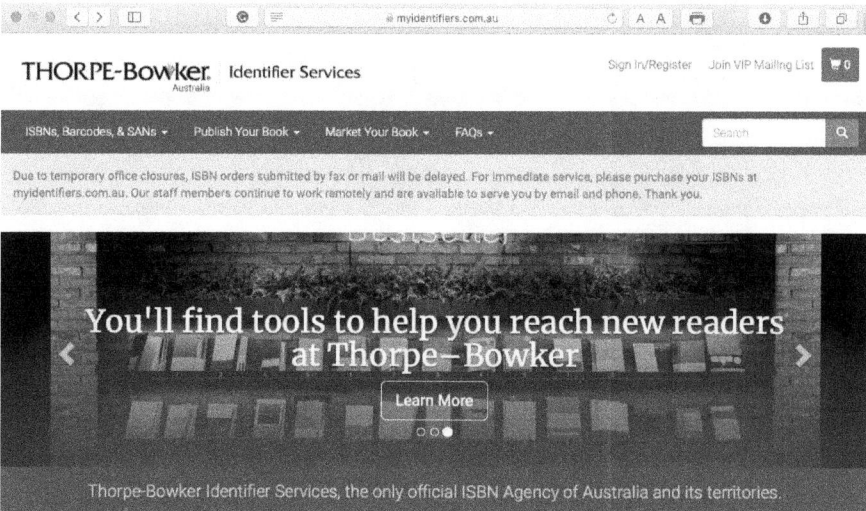

THORPE-Bowker. Australia Identifier Services

Sign In/Register   Join VIP Mailing List   0

ISBNs, Barcodes, & SANs ▾   Publish Your Book ▾   Market Your Book ▾   FAQs ▾   Search

Due to temporary office closures, ISBN orders submitted by fax or mail will be delayed. For immediate service, please purchase your ISBNs at myidentifiers.com.au. Our staff members continue to work remotely and are available to serve you by email and phone. Thank you.

You'll find tools to help you reach new readers at Thorpe–Bowker

Learn More

Thorpe-Bowker Identifier Services, the only official ISBN Agency of Australia and its territories.

ISBN (International Standard Book Number)

ISBNs help books get *discovered!*

Purchasing an ISBN is a big step toward ensuring your book's commercial success. An ISBN can help readers find and purchase your book because it identifies the book's specific format, edition, and publisher. Also, the ISBN:

THIS BIT IS FUN. I've taken heaps of screen grabs.

You'll need to register first, so click the words 'Sign In/Register'.

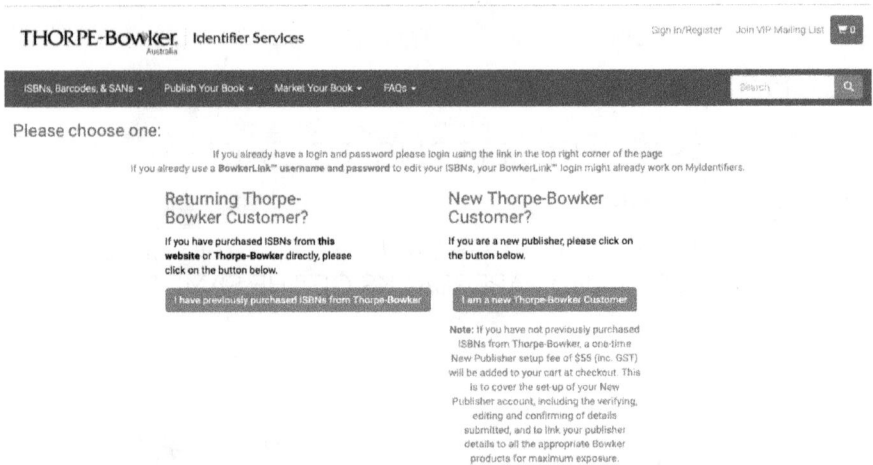

Take

Your

Time

Don't rush this part, as it's important. This is a time-intensive procedure, so please slow down and take your time.

You will spend half an hour filling out a form on the internet, which relies on decent download and upload speeds. I hope you have good network connection and patience aplenty. I'll take you through the process via a series of screen shots. Grab a cuppa and a snack.

Welcome to the Myidentifiers / Thorpe Bowker front page. Sign yourself in. In the next image, you can see I've signed in with my author email address and my top-secret password. (Which I created when I first registered.)

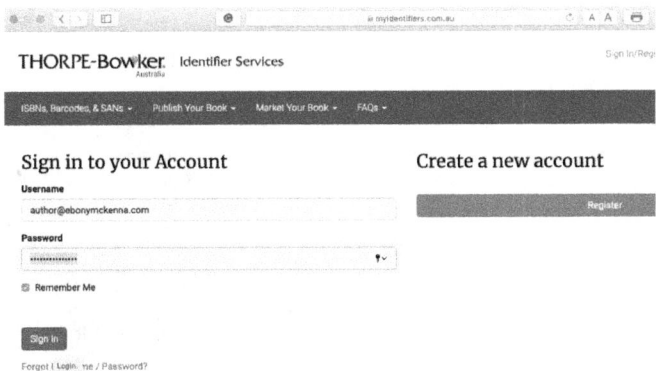

Once you sign in, select 'My Account' from that blue and white menu bar under the Thorpe Bowker logo in the next picture. It does look as if we've gone back to the start, but you'll see there is new text under the Thorpe Bowker logo, and it's my name! (It will be yours when you log in to your own account, obviously!)

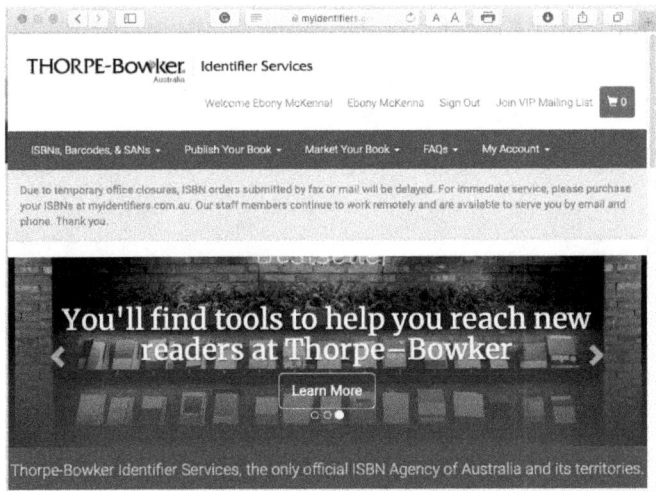

From the solid blue menu bar, select the white 'My Account' text, which opens a drop-down menu.

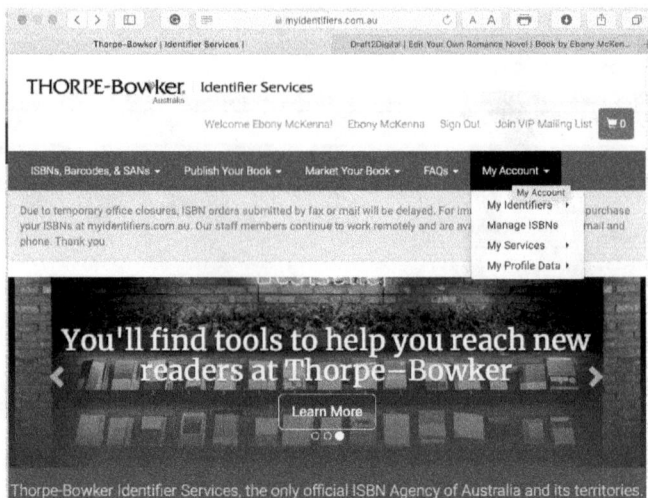

Select 'Manage ISBNs'

I have 120 ISBNs now, because I'm helping others through the publishing process these days. Plus, I'm writing heaps of shorter fiction which I am also publishing as ebook and then print, and at some point I'll get on to audio.

At the top of this list is the old title, Get Your Book Into Australian Libraries.

Guess what? As I've changed the book's name, and updating the content, I will need to assign new ISBNs. That's on my to-do list!

OK, let's get look at how we assign an ISBN to a book.

For this demonstration, I clicked on the second title (with the red incomplete cross-mark) *The Girl and The Ghost.*

I've filled in some but not all the details. You don't have to fill in every single detail, just the most important ones with the red asterisks. (However, the more information you do give, the more information library suppliers will have.)

The essential sections have red asterisks. Everything else is something you can fill in later if you want to.

GLITCH AHEAD

If you copy and paste your book's description/blurb into the Main Description section on this form, you'll need to scroll through and put in spaces after full stops at the paragraph returns. I'm not sure why the spaces vanish in a copy and paste, they just do.

If there's something you're not sure of, click on the grey question mark next to each section for an explanation.

After each page, click on the 'save' button to save the details, then click onto the next section and fill that out.

Format and Size

Medium

	Audio
	Digital
Format	E-Book
	Packs & Multimedia
Format Detail(s	Print
Selected	Video
	Other
Format Details	

Sidebar: Title & Cover / Contributors / Format & Size / Sales & Pricing

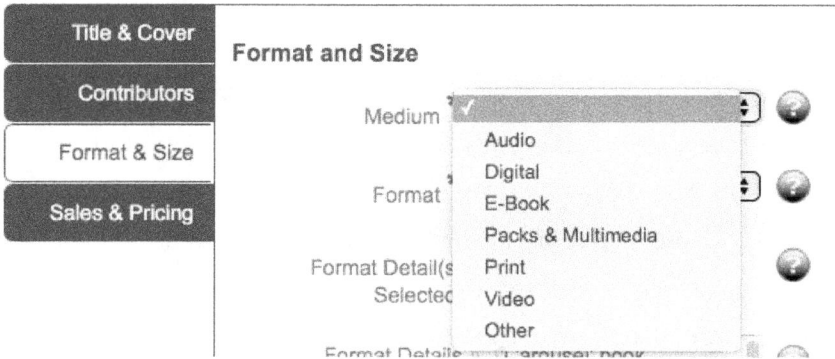

As my example is for a paperback, I've selected paperback on the 'Format and Size' page. If you're assigning an ISBN to an ebook, you'll need to select ebook.

When you're finished, make sure you click the 'submit' button on the bottom of the 'Sales and Pricing' page.

When you go back to the screen listing your ISBNs you'll get a yellow marker next to the title, showing that the title is being processed.

	Title		ISBN-13	Format	Cover	Barcode	Book Sales Widget
	1918-ish	Clone	978-0-9953839-0-8	Paperback	Change	Buy Barcode	
	The Girl and The Ghost	Clone	978-0-9953839-6-8	Paperback	Change	Buy Barcode	
	The Summer of Shambles	Clone	978-0-9953839-1-3	Paperback	Change	Buy Barcode	
	The Autumn Palace	Clone	978-0-9953839-2-0	Paperback	Change	Buy Barcode	
	The Winter of Magic	Clone	978-0-9953839-3-7	Paperback	Change	Buy Barcode	
	The Spring Revolution	Clone	978-0-9953839-4-4	Paperback	Change	Buy Barcode	

How cool was that? You just assigned your first (of many!) ISBNs.

The reason you fill all these details in at this point is because bookstore 'bots' on the internet search for details of your title to display on their websites. These bots can grab all the information about your book titles from the POD printers as well, but it's good to have things registered and official.

Make sure the details are as consistent as possible. If you're writing romantic time travel, then you want to make sure the words 'fiction, romance, time travel' appear next to your book in every retail and publishing outlet. In other words, get these pages right on myidentifiers, and copy and paste them everywhere else. Consistency is key - especially when it comes to library suppliers ordering your book and registering with Lending Rights.

Thorpe Bowker / myidentifiers is a handy resource for libraries and library suppliers. It's often their 'go to' resource for looking up authors and their books. You'll see where there is space to fill in the year of the author's birth - and death in the case of some authors (whose publishers fill out the forms for them, obviously.)

Side note: Often your book details will appear before the book cover does. I'm not sure why this happens.
It's as if book covers are the lost luggage of the literary world.

Oooh, before I forget. Nielsen Book Scan is a place librarians and library suppliers often visit as well. It's an excellent idea to get your book titles listed in here:

http://www.nielsenbookscan.com.au

Guess who's got two thumbs and hasn't registered her books yet? This gal!

Yeah, I really need to get on to that as well.

CHAPTER 5

THE COST OF PRINT RUNS
AND POSTAGE COSTS

THIS IS where your brain really gets a work-out. Up until now, it's been 'fill out this form, fill out that form.'

Now you need to do some maths and work out your print book pricing, because this is a business and you want to make a profit out of this exercise.

Whichever printing company you're using, play around with their printing price calculators. Grab a notebook and travel back to high school business maths and all that time you spent looking out the window instead of – Oops, talking about myself again.

OK

When you're looking at printing options, often the printers will have a help page or calculator on their website, so you can work out how much things will cost ahead of time.

Here are some of the helpful pricing calculators from Ingram Spark. (You'll find these by clicking the HELP button on their website.)

As an exercise, I put a 200-page 6x9 paperback into their calculator.

As we can see in the previous two images, the total cost of this print run would be $178.84.

Divide this by 30 books = $5.96 per book.

Not bad!

Playing around with this calculator will give me more options. If I order more books the price per book could come down by a few cents each, which all helps. If I make the font bigger in the book file, there will be more pages and so the cost per book will rise.

You want to get the unit price per book down, because you're up for a stack of extra costs straight after printing:

POSTAGE

It's very important to think about how much your book will weigh. The more pages, the more it weighs. (Ingram Spark have weight calculators as well.)

A 5x8inch book (which is a regular-sized paperback) will fit in a pre-paid 'Medium C5' envelope from the post office. You can buy these in 10 packs for about $25. That makes them $2.50 each. The maximum weight for these envelopes is 500g.

Which means, if you're posting books individually across Australia, you need to factor in an extra $2.50 per book into your cost price.

However, if the book is more than 250 pages, it won't fit in that envelope. It will be too fat. At this point you either think about reducing the font size of your book, or you go back and edit it one more time to reduce page count.

If you're making a 6x9inch book, which is the size of a *trade paperback*, then you'll need to step up to the 'Large C4 envelope', which is $46.80 for a pack of 10. This is for letters up to 500g and maximum thickness of 20mm.

The stamp's price is not printed on the pre-paid envelope. So once you buy them, if the price goes up (which it will) you're still good.

Go to this webpage and work out some calculations https://auspost.com.au/sending/send-within-australia/compare-letter-services/regular-letters-cards and also have a look at pre-paid satchels while you're at it.

It used to be different prices for sizes and weights. Now all pre-paid satchels can handle up to 5kg, and they're priced purely on the size.

Play around with the printing price calculators and also play around with formatting your book – you may find a 5x8 paperback is 300 pages, but if you change this format to 6x9, it comes in at 250 pages. That could make a difference to your profit margins.

PRINTING PRICE HACK:

If you price your books higher, you'll be able to offer a deeper discount, such as 55% (trades love this). Then when you approach the library suppliers, you can offer them a choice - 55% discount if they order directly from the printer (ie, Ingram etc) or 40% discount if they order from you (to cover postage.)

THOSE OF US WITH TRADITIONAL AND SMALL PRINT PUBLISHERS:

Authors are usually able to buy their titles directly from their publisher for 'author price'. This won't be counted as a sale, but you'll be able to buy them for only a little more than cost price.

If your publisher is in Australia, you'll be up for local postage (which could be considerable.)

Overseas publishers might not charge as much for postage as they may have a special deal with their country's postal service.

In any case, contact your publisher and let them know you're keen to market your books to Australian libraries.

If the publisher is overseas, they'll be happy for you to do this, as it will create interest in you as an author and they'll see you doing promotions.

If the publisher is Australian, they will be delighted as – get this – Australian publishers also get Lending Rights! It's free money for them, and it can only happen after the author registers for Lending Rights anyway. You'll be doing them a favour and yourself a favour. (This is also why it's super important self-published authors are listed as the publisher because they'll get extra Lending Rights.)

BUT your Australian small publisher may already have a deal in place with a library supplier, so what you need to do is contact them and ask them as nicely as possible about the best way you can get your books into libraries. You want to appear helpful and positive, and show them that you're keen to get your name out there.

If your publisher makes their titles available to library suppliers at trade discount rates, you won't need to worry about pricing or postage as your publisher has this in hand. (Even if they're not very good at it, which is always a possibility.) The key here is not to blunder in and embarrass your publisher or attempt to reinvent the wheel. Because we're all being incredibly professional about this.

No resting on your laurels, published authors. You still need to contact library suppliers to let them know where to get your book, and you still need to contact libraries and let them know about your book. It's lots of self-promotion, in a good way. So stay tuned, I'll have lots of work for you to do next chapter.

So much work!

CHAPTER 6

AUTHORS WITH INTERNATIONAL PUBLISHERS

IF YOU'RE PUBLISHED INTERNATIONALLY, but you haven't been picked up by an Australian publisher, you have a couple more steps.

1. Send a copy of your book to the National Library of Australia (NLA). This is because your book already has an ISBN, but it's not from Australia, so there won't be a MARC record. Sending a copy to the NLA will get your title, name, ISBN and book details 'into the system' so to speak.
2. Negotiate with your publisher about buying author copies here - or
3. Check which printer your publisher is using. This is so the library suppliers know where they can purchase copies of your book.

CHAPTER 7

PRICING YOUR BOOKS

HOW MUCH TO CHARGE FOR PAPERBACKS AND EBOOKS?

NOW WE GET DOWN to the pointy end – What price do you put on your book to make it attractive to library suppliers and libraries, while also delivering you a little profit?

EBOOKS

This is super easy. Load your title into Draft To Digital and select Publish To Library Services.

The tricky part here is pricing. It must be $1.99 US to qualify for these lending services. Hoopla for some reason have only accepted one of my books so far (*The Girl and The Ghost*, yeah!) and as you can see from the warning note in the next image, they don't allow price changes.

But it's pretty awesome that we can get our ebooks into library services all over the world for a few clicks. If only it was that easy for print!

Library Services

Library services provide a catalog of available ebooks to library staff. Each library chooses which of those books to make available to their patrons. The library may either purchase the book through a "Cost Per Checkout" model or "One Copy/One User" Learn more.

Library Price (USD):

1.99

Library Services
These services allow members to check out ebooks on temporary loan.

Name	Projected Royalties	Special Considerations
OverDrive	One Copy, One User: $0.93 Cost Per Checkout: $0.46	
Bibliotheca	One Copy, One User: $0.93	
Baker & Taylor	One Copy, One User: $0.93	
BETA TESTING Hoopla	Cost Per Checkout: $0.26	Hoopla does not allow price changes. Your book is listed for $1.99 and this price cannot be changed, but you can delist at any time.

PRINT BOOKS

Let's say I set the retail price of my paperback novel at $15.95.

Side note: When I say 'print' or 'paperback' I also mean 'hardback'. You can have large print too. I'm just using the words print or paperback as shorthand for 'your printed book which is made from paper and cardboard and glue'. OK and sometimes there's stitching as well.

The RRP needs to include GST at some point. Personally, I'm not registered to collect GST, so I can't charge it (oh gawd, I'm talking taxes, somebody shoot me.) But I do have an ABN because I'm a professional.

If a library supplier sells my book for $15.95 it will include $1.45 GST, which must go to the government. (ie, $14.50 + 10% GST of $1.45 = $15.95)

(To find the GST portion of your end price, take the total price and divide by 11. That gives you 10% GST. It's like sorcery or something. Or, if you do it the other way round, take your base price and add 10%. Ie. If you're selling for $16.00, then add $1.60 to make it $17.60.)

Maths time!

If this $15.95 RRP book costs $5.96 each to print, so we're down to $9.99. (Hardbacks do cost more to print, but they are also much more durable and will cope with being borrowed more times, so you can set the price higher to reflect this.)

If I directly sell this book directly to readers, which I sometimes do, I get a tidy profit. Well done me!

But we're not always directly selling (especially during covid when all the booky events were cancelled). We're selling to library *suppliers*, and they'd like to make a little money for their troubles too.

No, you can't sell directly to public libraries. Most of them simply can't do it. Public libraries are local government entities who are spending public money, so they can only purchase from authorised suppliers. School libraries might make an exception, but they too have to answer to their school councils and keep to their budgets, so they would most likely not be able to buy directly from the author either.

Let's look at this again, offering the library supplier a reasonable discount.

A common discount they'd be interested in would be 40% off the RRP.

40% of $15.95 = $6.38

So, the $15.95 RRP minus the $6.38 discount = $9.57

$9.57 - $5.96 (the cost of the book) = $3.61

$3.61 is still OK as 'profit', but then you have to factor in postage, and postage eats into your profits.

Postage: $2.60

Hooray, you get $1 profit!

This is why it's important to play with your retail price and see if you can offer the higher 55% discount and still make a few bucks. As I said in the last chapter, I'm offering 55% trade discount to library suppliers when they place orders with Ingram Spark, and only 40% when placed directly with me. I've already had a reply from one supplier to say, 'thanks for that, we'll order from IS.'

It's a bonus for me as I then have less paperwork and can focus on writing the next book instead of ordering and packaging and posting books all over the country.

I am a big fan of the 'set and forget' style of getting things done.

WHERE'S THE PROFIT?

In the Lending Rights!

In years to come, as long as you have more than 50 printed books on library shelves across the country, each printed book you have on that library shelf will earn you about $2 royalty per copy with Public Lending Right (PLR), and you keep getting that PLR for **each year** those books remain on the shelves. Plus, you'll get 30-50c per book as the listed publisher as well.

Educational Lending Rights operate in a similar way.

WHAT ABOUT IMMEDIATE PROFIT? I'D LIKE SOME OF THAT PLEASE.

The other option is to increase the RRP of your book so that you can offer deeper trade discounts.

I bought Anh Do's *The Happiest Refugee* for $32.99 RRP! I bought it from a regular book store and it's on my son's reading list for English (so I bet Anh is extra happy, as are his publishers.)

It's 6 x 9.25 inches in size (15.24cm x 23.495 cm) and 232 pages. With a 55% trade discount, it would have cost the bookstore about $14.85 each. There is a block of colour photos in the middle, which would add to printing costs, but I think each print edition would average about $7.50 each. (So if Anh's on a 10% net royalty, he'll be getting $1.48 per book sale, ps.)

My novels are 5 x 8 (12.7cm x 20.32) and average 250 pages and I'm suddenly thinking I should charge WAY more than $15.95 RRP!

(Update - printing costs have increased substantially since this was first published, so I'm now charging $19.95)

If you think the market will cope, and you've got a cracking story and the covers are magnificently beautiful, then go for it and charge a higher RRP so you can offer a bigger discount without crippling your bottom line.

Just remember: the more pages, the more it weighs, the more it will cost to print.

Visit a general bookstore and see what their prices are for books that are like yours.

Don't compare prices at Big W/Target/K-mart

though, their books are heavily, *heavily* discounted and are often 'loss leaders'. You will not be able to compete with them.

EBOOK PRICING

Libraries have limited budgets and they need books that will stand the rigours of multiple lendings. Which is why you need to use a good printer with a great reputation.

Ebooks don't have this issue and **just about every library across the country offers ebook lending**. Which is excellent for discoverability.

But their budgets are still limited. If they see your book is available to libraries for $9.95, but the general public can get it for $2.99, they might not want your book at all. Yes, the higher library price will make up for the loss of some sales, but your aim is to get your books out there and get them in front of readers' eyeballs. Higher prices for libraries could hamper that ambition. Consider lowering the library price and possibly raising the general sale price and see how you go.

Back Matter

As I said, we don't have lending rights for ebooks and audio *at the moment*, so if you're getting ebooks and audio into libraries, it's vitally important to have back matter that shows the reader who you are, what other books you have, what awards you've won etc.

Put in your website and newsletter signup link in the back. Not every reader will sign up, but every now and then one of them will and they will become fans.

Do not put in direct buy links to specific retailers in your back matter, because that can trigger automatic file rejection from retailers.

Ask readers to leave reviews, but don't mention specific places. Phrases like 'please leave a review on Amazon' in your back matter (even when it's not a link) will see the file rejected. The reason it gets rejected is that it upsets all the other retailers who hate seeing the word Amazon in your book (unless you're referring to the geographic region in Brazil).

TROUBLE SHOOTING

If your ebook is in KU, that means it must be exclusive to KU for the rest of the 3 month term that it's in for. You can't list your ebook into library services - or anywhere else, like as a free or even paid download from your own website - while it's in KU.

Once the exclusive KU term is up, that's when you can put it into libraries. But once it's in libraries, you can't then add it to KU. You'll have to take it out before you put your title back into KU.

Small Press authors

If you're published with a small press, and your book is available only as an ebook, ask your publisher if your titles are being distributed through Overdrive and other library services. That might be all you need to do for ebooks at this stage. However, if you're interested in print runs, ask if your publisher will bring your books out in print – or ask if they'll give you permission to do it yourself. (Check your contract, you may already have the print rights.)

If you're printed with a small press publisher, ask your publisher where library suppliers can order your books and what the trade discount is set to. The library suppliers will want to know what the discount is.

As I've already mentioned, there are no Lending Right for ebooks and audio (at this stage), which means your ebook-only publisher might not be interested in helping you get your books into libraries. They might even see their ebooks in libraries as a negative, as selling one ebook to a library could be regarded as lost sales to all the people who borrow it instead of buy it.

This is something you'll need to negotiate with your publisher. However, if they have paperbacks, then I'm sure they'll be happy to have those in libraries, as Australian publishers will get those Lending Rights down the track.

PUBLISHERS LOVE LENDING RIGHTS

But, it has to be the author who registers the books. (I don't make the rules). In other words, the Australian publisher gets free money from all the work you're doing. Harrah!

Then again, they took a punt on you and have worn all the costs so far, so it's only right they should get a little extra, down the track.

IF YOUR PUBLISHER IS OVERSEAS:

They may have a similar PLR situation in their country, but as you're not a resident of that country, you can't claim it. I had stacks of books in British Libraries but I couldn't get anything for them as I'm not a resident. Boo Hoo, sucks to be me. But also, the publisher here in Australia, who picked up my book, managed to get my books into plenty of libraries, so, swings and roundabouts.

If your publisher is overseas, contact them about your plans to get the books into libraries here in Australia. Be open and encouraging. Negotiate with them to get a good supply of books, whether directly from a printer or from you. When orders come in, you'll want to fulfil them quickly, so the library supplier recognises that you're a 'good egg' and you're easy to deal with.

YOUR CHECKLIST FOR PART ONE

Have I given you enough work to do?

- Buy ISBNs
- Create a publisher name or use your author name
- Assign one ISBN to each format of your book
- Publish your books (or get ready to publish them)
- Select Overdrive as a distribution option with your ebook distributor
- Work out book prices for your print runs, whether self-published or if you're with a small press
- If you're traditionally published, contact your publisher to discuss your plans to get your titles into Australian libraries
- Work out your postage costs and try not to cry
- Cry anyway

Next, we'll look at all the library suppliers across Australia, how to contact them in a completely professional manner and how to fill in even more online forms!

Plus, it will soon be time to register for those Lending Rights I keep talking about.

PART 2

LEARNING ALL ABOUT LENDING RIGHTS

CHAPTER 8

GETTING READY TO EARN ROYALTIES

ARE you ready for another stack of work? Off we go. In part two we'll be:

- Judging books by their covers
- Learning about Lending Rights
- Registering for Lending Rights and filling out online forms
- Putting together a list of Australian library suppliers (for print books)
- Investigating options for ebooks
- Contacting library suppliers - via email and/or by filling in their online forms (yay, more online forms!)
- Creating your own tax invoices (excel spreadsheets galore!)
- Feeling incredibly satisfied that we are nearly there

The online forms will absolutely do your head in after a

while, (ooops, talking about myself again) but as you fill them in, you'll make brilliant progress in making your books available to libraries, and that's what this is all about.

Once again I'll be here in the trenches with you.

For those of us with ebooks/ audio only (and no print yet) you get to snooze somewhat through this part - but please do read through all of it because it might inspire you to venture into print.

Sure, Lending Rights don't apply to digital - YET - but it's still important to know all of this stuff and be ready to apply for Lending Rights the moment ebooks get the green light.

So, let's get to work.

CHAPTER 9

JUDGING A BOOK BY ITS COVER

WE ALL DO IT

WHETHER YOU CAN ADMIT it or not, we do judge books by their covers.

Personally, you may bristle at this suggestion, determined that you don't; that you always judge a book on its merits. To that I say, 'Good for you.'

The reason you perhaps take the time to pick up a book – regardless of the cover – and flip it over to read the blurb, even if it's written poorly – and then perhaps open the first page to have a look at the opening few paragraphs that may or may not be very well written . . . is that word starting with T:

Time.

Librarians and library suppliers are busy people who don't have time to mess around. That means we can't waste their time.

Leave your creative writer brain behind and become a complete professional (remember, they can't see the curry stains on your pyjamas).

Being professional starts with an awesome cover. A cover that says, 'This book will be an excellent use of your time.'

Spend some of your time in a book store or library, looking at covers. Go to Amazon and scroll through the top 100 in your favourite category. Be as brutally judgemental as possible. (Privately.) Look at the covers with a critical eye, but also listen to your heart. Does the cover make you sigh? Does it elicit a mood?

Have a look inside the book, at the copyright page and see if the author has acknowledged who created the cover for them. Then look up that cover designer and introduce yourself.

If it's an indie author, they will often acknowledge the cover creator. If it's a big publisher, they might not specifically name the designer, which is annoying.

Check out TheBookDesigner.com and have a scroll through the monthly book cover awards. Some of them are extraordinary and some are just . . . oh dear. If you see a cover you love, think about the feeling it evokes. Magic, emotions, love, passion, fear, intrigue, horror etc. Get a few covers you love and see if your designer can make you a cover that will evokes those.

WARNING:

Don't completely rip off the artwork. If the cover you love is already pretty famous (or even if it's not) don't make your cover too similar. Not only is it bad form, you could find yourself in legal trouble with copyright claims etc.

Allow me to present the craziest story from YA Twitter of all time:

The cover art on *Handbook for Mortals* bore a striking resemblance to, *The Knife Thrower* by artist Gill Del-Mace.

Check it out here.

Trust me, you don't want to end up becoming a punchline for shady behaviour. If you see something you love and want a cover 'like that', just go with the general *vibe*, OK.

Don't do it yourself. Trust me, unless you're a graphic designer and you really, *REALLY* know what you're doing, do not design the cover yourself.

OK, yes, some people can design a book cover themselves, but it's rare. And you don't want to end up featured in Lousy Book Covers. Go ahead and waste some time over there. I'm sorry for the metaphorical punch in the face.

HOW TO FIND A COVER DESIGNER?

Ask around. If you see a stunning cover on facebook or twitter, ask the author who the cover artist is.

Post questions on social media ask the 'hive mind' for recommendations.

If you're after something super affordable, try checking out websites with ready made ebook covers for about $100 US each. It will give you an idea of what's out there. Again, be brutally judgemental - this is your book baby we're talking about - and see what appeals and appalls.

Recently, I've used US-based Fiona Jayde Designs (For *Robyn and the Hoodettes*) and Australia's own Lana Pecherczyk (for *The Girl & The Ghost*).

Fiona Jayde does brilliant historical covers, including some stunners for Alison Stuart's historical romance books.

Lana is amazing with contemporary and crime, and is also an incredible artist herself. She has a great eye for graphic design. I realise that by naming Lana, I feel like she'll be snowed under with work and she won't have time to any more of my covers.

YOUR COVER NEEDS TO WORK FOR YOU (NOT AGAINST YOU).

The cover will be the first thing librarians see, when you send them a completely professional email (with the sell sheet) about your book. It will also be one of the first things library suppliers see as well. Library suppliers also make their own promotional material to send out to libraries, so the more gorgeous and genre-appropriate your cover, the better your sales are likely to be.

SPINE SPACE

I nearly forgot. Now that your print books are heading towards library shelves, spare a thought for the librarian who needs to catalogue your book. Make space near the base of the spine for a sticker or two. You want readers to find your name quickly, and if your name goes all the way down the spine, there will be a sticker over it, which makes reading your name more difficult.

Spend a little time looking along a library shelf to see what I mean. You might never have noticed this before, but you will now.

CHAPTER 10

REGISTERING FOR LENDING RIGHTS

THIS IS THE GOOD STUFF

LET'S dispel a quick myth that never wants to die. Authors don't receive a royalty every time their book is borrowed from a library. The royalties from book lending is paid once a year, and it's based on the total number of physical books on library shelves. If they're regularly borrowed, they'll stay on the shelves for years. If they're not borrowed, the libraries will most likely sell them to make space for newer books that will get borrowed.

An author needs to earn about $100 (this may change) from about 50 copies of the *one title* in order to earn Lending Rights for that book.

Lending Rights came about because of a concerted effort from the Australian Society of Authors (the ASA). Public Lending Rights came into effect in 1975, and Educational Lending Rights in 2000. The ASA is actively campaigning to have Digital Lending Rights (ebooks and audio books) included.

I'm so grateful to the ASA for this campaign, and I am proud to be a member. You should totally join up, if you're not already.

Lending Rights are managed by the Australian Government **Department** ~~of Communications and Arts.~~ **of Infrastructure, Transport, Regional Development and Communications**

Office for the Arts

Australian Government
Department of Infrastructure, Transport,
Regional Development and Communications
Office for the Arts

I'm not crying, you're crying.

Lending Rights hail from the Public Lending Right Act, 1985. Here's the important bit:

2A Objects of Act

(a) to make payments to Australian creators of books, and to publishers of books in Australia, in recognition of their loss of income from their books being available for loan from, or for use in, public lending libraries in Australia; and

(b) to support the enrichment of Australian culture by encouraging Australian persons to create books and by encouraging publishers to publish books in Australia.

How about that? It's there to compensate us, and it's there to encourage us to make awesome books and get them into libraries! So really, we should all be doing our patriotic duty as much as possible!

To familiarise yourself, go to this page (as of May 21, 2021, the link still worked!)

https://www.arts.gov.au/funding-and-support/lending-rights

and spend time reading about how Lending Rights work and, most importantly, whether you're eligible. If you're the co-author, you'll split the Lending Rights with your fellow authors. (But only a maximum of five authors.)

Australian citizens and residents are eligible. But guess what? You MUST have an ISBN and it must be officially recorded in an official database - which is why we spent all that time making sure we bought proper ISBNs and they are registered to us as the publisher (where applicable) in an official place of record (ie, Thorpe Bowker or Neilsen Bookscan.)

Now we are going to fill in some online forms. I first registered for Lending Rights in 2010. I've previously filled in the details of who I am, and filled in my bank account details.

BUT I also need to register now as a publisher, so claims for the new editions of the Ondine novels come to me as author and as the publisher, while the older editions from Hardie Grant Egmont still come to me as the author, but to HGE as the publisher. (They have different ISBNs, so that solves any issues there.)

First timers to Lending Rights, start with this online form here:

https://lendingrights.arts.gov.au

The front page will have these two boxes in the top right corner.

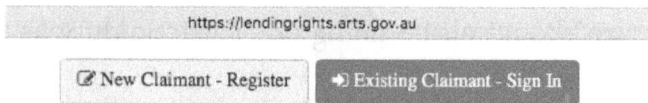

https://lendingrights.arts.gov.au

☑ New Claimant - Register   ➟ Existing Claimant - Sign In

If you're a brand new claimant, click the Register box for new claimants.

If you're a returning claimant, click the 'Sign In' box.

Now, we have some deadlines that must be met.

Title claims for the 2022-23 programs need to be lodged by 31 March 2022 for eligible books or editions you have not claimed. You may submit title claims for books published between 1 January 2016 and 31 December 2021.

The deadline is always March 31 for the books published the year before. If you miss the deadline, that's OK, you have five years to register your book and you'll still be eligible.

Remember: It's not retrospective. So if your book was published in 2015 but you didn't register until 2019, then you've missed those years of royalties. However, you will continue to collect royalties for as many years as your books are on shelves (in sufficient numbers) in libraries.

If this is all too tricky (and it can be confusing) There are helplines you can call, so someone can hold your hand and walk you through it.

UPDATE! They are so helpful! I had a call a couple of weeks ago from a lovely chap at the Lending Rights office. Yes, he called me! Guess what dopey thing I'd done? I'd registered as a publisher (for all my self-published books) and then hadn't filled in my titles! There was an issue with the connection between my registration as an author and publisher, which he fixed so quickly so they were linked, and off I went. Thank you!

MATCH YOUR CATEGORIES

Not only will you need to make sure the ISBN is spot on, and your titles are correctly matched; you'll need to make sure your book description is the same. Otherwise Lending Rights will have a fit and you'll get 'computer says no' treatment. Maintain consistency with correct titles, description, ISBN, publisher, keywords/categories. If there's a mismatch, Lending Rights will query your 'MARC'. MARC stands for **Ma**chine **R**eadable **C**ataloguing record, and you can burn your noggin reading about it.

You will need to give Lending Rights your bank account details. The money is electronically deposited once a year. In late May or early June each year. The money is considered taxable income, PS, so make sure you keep good records.

The website is often slow to load, especially when it's close to the deadline for registering books. If the slow speed drives you mad, log off and have a cup of tea (or something stronger) and come back later and try again.

Reminder: you have several years to register each title and its corresponding ISBN, but you only get paid for the years **after** *you register (it doesn't work retrospectively). If your book came out in 2019 but you only registered for it in 2021, you won't see money for those two years between 2019 and 2021, only the years that follow. The earlier you register, the more you'll get.*

When you're the author AND the publisher, you are eligible for *publisher payments* as well. It's not as much as the author gets - I think it averages out to 30 or 50c or something - but it's a lovely little top-up and you deserve it.

That's is why you need to get a proper ISBN where you can be listed as the publisher. Noooooow it's all making sense, right?

Another thing about Lending Rights. They are broken up into separate Public Lending Rights (for public libraries) and Educational Lending Rights (for school libraries). You need to 'earn' a minimum $100 in royalties for each title, about 50 copies, otherwise you get nothing. (Here, have a tissue.) My most recent statement showed only 10 copies of one of my titles, so I earned nothing for that one. (But I had nearly 300 of another title, so that made up for it!)

What's worse, Lending Rights for that low-number don't 'roll over' to the following year either.

I also wouldn't be surprised if they raise this minimum to $150 soon. Grumble, mumble.

The next image is really important. It's your Title Claim.

55

Enter ONE ISBN (even though there's space for five)

Title Claim

Creator title claim for : 309291

Please note:
- to be eligible to receive a payment, you must be entitled to receive a royalty payment for the sale of this book.
- No MARC record books, books older than five years, EBooks, online resources, magazines, serials, CDs, audio books, activity books, single use books (e.g. workbooks, colouring-in books) are ineligible to claim.

Are you self publishing this title claim?   `Yes` ⬍ *

If you are an eligible creator and publishing your own book, then you will need to register as a self publisher. You will also need to submit a Title Claim for both your Creator and Publisher IDs.

Details of ISBNs for this edition of the title	ISBN	Book Form	Year of Publication (yyyy)
	9780995383981	Printed ⬍	2016 ⬍
		Printed ⬍	⬍
		Printed ⬍	⬍
		Printed ⬍	⬍
		Printed ⬍	⬍

`Click here to validate book details`

ISBN validation is complete.

Book Title	Robyn and the Hoodettes *
Publisher's Name	Ebony McKenna *
Place of Publication	[Australia] *
Your name or a pseudonym as shown on the title page	Ebony McKenna
What was your contribution to this title?	Author ⬍ *
Do you receive royalties from the sale of this title?	Yes ⬍ *
What is your percentage entitlement to the royalties?	100 (%) *

Payments are calculated based on the royalty split of each eligible creator. If you are the sole creator, enter your royalty split as 100%. If there is more than one eligible creator, list your royalty split out of 100%. For example, if there are two creators, and you receive 7.5% and the other receives 2.5% you enter 75%. If there are three creators who receive an equal royalty split, then you enter 33.33% For Self

Dang, would you look at that? I've put the wrong year in for Robyn and the Hoodettes. 2016 is when it came out as an ebook, and then the print book was 2017. Gah! But never fear, I can contact the Lending Rights folks and sort it out. In any case, I'm not expecting vast amounts from this title straight away, and I hardly think one year out is going to cause too many headaches. I hope! But in any case, if you do make a mistake, contact them via the help number or the help email, and let them know.

As the sole author, **I am entitled to 100% of the royalty for my book.**

This often confuses some authors who mix this section up with the royalty rate they're getting from their *publisher* for book sales, which can be as miserable as 4% but is usually somewhere around 10%.

For a Lending Right claim, you're getting 100%. Unless you've co-authored. If there are two of you, you're claiming 50% each and if there are 3 of you 33% and so on. However, if one of you has done the bulk of the work, then you may need to claim a 60-40 or 70-30 split instead.

The smallest amount you can claim is 20%. **This means there can be no more than five overall contributors**. This could be five authors, or four authors and an illustrator etc. I'm pretty sure it does not include the editor, unless the editor is also a direct contributor. (For example, an editor who also contributes a story in an anthology.) If you're not sure, then please contact Lending Rights to get confirmation.

Once you're done, click the teeensy little 'I agree' box and submit your claim!

The sooner you get on to it, the better. My first book, *Ondine*, hit shelves in 2010. I registered straight away and started getting ELR (Education Lending Right) and PLR (Public Lending Right) in 2012 and it was marvellous. Close to $500 for just one book across both lending rights. I was rapt. In 2011 I added *The Autumn Palace* into Lending Rights and from 2013 my royalties grew. The royalties stayed high for several years, which showed me just how valuable Lending Rights are. (It also proved my books were on library shelves for years. Books don't stay on the shelves if they're not getting borrowed.)

My point being, yes, this is a lot of work. Loads of forms to fill in and you might not end up getting all that much for a few years. BUT it's there, it builds every year, so you may as well take your slice of the pie.

CHAPTER 11

DEADLINES FOR LENDING RIGHTS

WHEN YOU REGISTER for Lending Rights, especially for books that might be a few years old or previously published, you may find the book is too old to register.

Basically you have five years in which to register your book, and if it was published more than five years ago, you can't register for Lending Rights. (Even if that particular book is still on library shelves.)

The answer to this situation is to publish a new edition, with a new ISBN. Then you'll need to start the process of marketing that new edition to library suppliers and libraries again.

Once your new book is registered for Lending Rights, it doesn't 'expire', as long as it's still on library shelves in enough numbers.

As an example, my books that were published in 2010 were still earning Lending Rights in 2020! The numbers on shelves declined as those books get borrowed and damaged or lost over the years. (Or not borrowed so the library gets rid of them to make way for new books.)

You have until March 31 to register books published in the previous year.

There is no penalty for registering 'early', so you may as well register the books soon after they're published, then you don't have to worry about it again. You don't need to keep registering each year, either.

Remember, you can only register book titles for Lending Rights once you've registered the ISBN in a recognised database, like Thorpe Bowker.

CHAPTER 12

AUSTRALIAS BIG LIBRARY SUPPLIERS

THE BIG PLAYERS in public library suppliers in Australia are:

James Bennett - NSW based. Here's their information page for small and indie publishers. (That's us!)

https://www.bennett.com.au/publisherservices.cfm

Peter Pal - Qld based

http://www.peterpal.com.au

WestBooks - WA based

http://www.westbooks.com.au

ALS Library Services - SA based

https://www.alslib.com.au

DLS - Vic based

http://www.dlsbooks.com

These are the big five I've been dealing with. (Along with some smaller suppliers and independent bookstores who sell directly into schools.)

In many cases, you'll need to send an email introducing your-self and your book titles. Once you introduce yourself, you'll need to fill in all their online information forms about each title. Huzzah, more online forms!

Although there's basically one big supplier in each state, they don't have a monopoly in those states. That means even if you've only made contact with James Bennett, they still supply books to libraries across Australia (and New Zealand).

My best relationship has been with ALS in South Australia. They are so completely lovely, and they're keen to hear from self-published authors. I used to fill in their new title forms, but now ALS has an online

Here's how it works:

- I visit a supplier's website
- Find and fill in the forms to register my books with them, along with ISBNs, covers, blurbs, dimensions, weight etc.
- Register the retail prices and the trade discounts they would receive - the pricing we worked out last part comes into effect here.
- Contact libraries directly and let them know my book is available from the proper suppliers.
- A few weeks later, the suppliers get orders from libraries. They either order directly from the printer or contact me via email with an order for books.

Here's where you need to get really organised (big shout out to everyone with ADHD. #TheStruggleIsReal)

You'll need to keep records of which companies you've contacted - and all the website logins and passwords to re-access when your next book comes out. The more work you do, and the less work they have to do, the more professional you will appear.

Take your time to look over these main five websites. Click on their pages to see what they do (they do a lot!). Once your books are in with these library suppliers, you're really on your way.

You're in the big time now!

You as the author still need to let the libraries know your books are available, so get ready to make sell sheets and be totes profesh about it.

Again, if you are with a small press and you want to make sure your books are available to libraries, check with your publisher to see what sales channels they are going to sell through (if it's in your contract) or ask your editor on which sales platforms your books are sold. Sorry if I'm repeating myself, but if you're with a small press you need to be businesslike and keep in contact - don't assume they'll do the work for you. (Note the problem - 'I'd like to be in libraries' - then give them the solution - 'I know how to do this, make it available in Overdrive' etc.)

Ebook suppliers:

You can access all of these 'big players' by selecting the library channels in either Smashwords or Draft 2 Digital.

- Bibliotheca - they run Cloud Library
- Baker and Taylor
- Overdrive

The other big one is Bolinda Digital - they provide audio and ebooks to libraries via their Borrow Box platform. Please visit my website for up-to-date links and information as this situation does change - and it will keep on changing.

CHAPTER 13

CONTACTING LIBRARY SUPPLIERS

THE FIRST CONTACT you'll have with a library supplier is online. As a new supplier, you'll need to have all your information at hand - your ABN, book details, banking details etc. You need an ABN so they can put you into their system as a supplier. Without an ABN, you're going to give them tax withholding headaches.

Australian business number (ABN) | Australian Taxation Office

If you're conducting business in Australia it's best to have an ABN. If you don't, other businesses have to withhold 47% (from 1 July 2017) from their payments to you. If you're required to register for GST you must get an ABN.

business / international-tax-for-business

/ foreign-residents-doing-business-in-australia

30-Jun-2017

Headaches, anyone?

GET AN ABN

If you don't have an ABN, it's easy to get one. Have your Tax File number handy and click on this link. And then cry at how slow everything is.

Obviously, if the library supplier is able to order directly from the printer, you won't need your ABN, but it's still handy to have one and they don't cost anything - and it's entirely possible the supplier will still want to order directly from you anyway.)

When you contact the library supplier, it will probably be via their 'contact us' email. So send them an email introducing yourself.

SAMPLE INTRO EMAIL

"Good Morning Peter Pal Team,

I'm [state your real name] an Australian author with [number of] books in print under the writing name of [my writing name].

[A paragraph here about your titles.] (Or something like this which shows you're a professional. Being kind and nice is always a good way to start, but let's not get too buttery.)

As a self-published author/author with a small press, I have a good supply of titles available at an attractive discount. Please see the attached images of my exciting new release/s (and attach a couple of .jpg files of your most recent book/books if you have them).

Please send me the form for new publication details and I shall complete them presently.

Yours faithfully,

my name here."

Obviously this is just a churned out letter and you will do a much better job when you come to do this for real. Each library supplier has their own New Publication Details forms to fill out - either an email address or an online form (in which case you can't attach images).

BIC CATEGORIES

BIC SUBJECT CATEGORIES

Use the BIC Subject Category Selection Tool (see http://editeur.dyndns.org/bic_categories) to assign at least one subject category to your work. Note that without subject category assignment your work will not be visible in any of the selection lists used by Peter Pal Library Supplier or our clients. If your work is related to a specific geographical region, be sure to select the appropriate BIC Geographic Qualifier to ensure that it known to be relevant to libraries in that region (e.g. 1MBFQ = Queensland).

BIC Subject Category #1

BIC Subject Category #2

BIC Subject Category #3

On the Peter Pal form they ask for BIC Categories. They also provide a link so you can make sure they're correct. For example, my 'Edit Your Own' books will fit the BIC of :

"CBW Writing and editing guides..."

The BIC categories are different to other library sorting categories. (And different again to some online retailer's seemingly arbitrary categories) But it's good to be across them. Again, take your time and click about, seeing which categories most closely fit your books.

CHAPTER 14

INVOICES

IF YOU'RE GOING TO HANDLE THE SALES YOURSELF

IT'S brilliant if library suppliers go straight to your printer to get stock, that way you don't have to handle the sales and invoices.

But if they do want to deal directly with you, get ready.

They will most likely email an order of books to you, but sometimes you'll get snail mail.

Get the order together and send it off promptly with your invoice.

Your invoice needs to include:

- ABN
- Date
- Library Supplier's Order Number (so they can match it to their ordering records.)
- Number of titles ordered and the ISBNs of those titles
- Full RRP cost of the books

- Cost of titles to the library supplier - including the discount
- Total cost the supplier needs to pay
- If you're registered for GST, put GST on it.
- If not, don't put GST.
- Provide your bank account details because you want to get paid, right?

If the order is for one book, make sure the book won't get damaged by wrapping it in paper or card first.

If sending a few books, wrap them together in something light but firm, such as a manilla folder, to keep them steady and protect them from bashing around into each other in transit.

If it's an order for ten or more books, then it might be best to send them directly from the printer - with the library supplier's address. If you do this, send the supplier an email explaining that the books will be coming directly from the printer. You won't be able to put your invoice in with those books, so email them your invoice and make sure all the details are there so they can match them up at their end.

Side Note: ALS has made an invoice template already, which automatically calculates discounts. GST and adds up the total.
Click Here.

It bears repeating, don't charge GST unless you're registered for it. Once you're registered, you have to charge GST for everything unless it's 'educational' which I assume is non-fiction maybe?

Don't charge extra postage unless you've previously stated

you'll be doing that. It's just a personal thing, but I like to know how much I'm up for when I buy things online, and I don't like surprises. That's why we did all the calculations earlier, so that you could include postage in the price of your books - or at least indicate what the postage would be.

YOUR CHECKLIST FOR PART TWO

You have a fair bit to go on with now.

- Make sure your covers are brilliant - chase down your favourite designers and get the best cover for your book.
- Register for Lending Rights.
- Draft a professional introduction for contacting library suppliers.
- Get an ABN (if you don't already have one).
- Create your own tax invoices and templates for when the orders come in.

Next part we'll be creating Sell Sheets and contacting libraries to let them know where they can order your books!

PART 3

PROMOTING YOUR BOOKS TO LIBRARIES

CHAPTER 15

SELL SHEETS

THIS PART WILL FOCUS on the vital tasks of making sell sheets to promote your books and making contact with public and school libraries (If your books are suitable for schools)

Our three important jobs this part are:

- Creating Sell sheets
- Creating Library lists
- Contacting Libraries

What is a sell sheet anyway?

It's a standard size (usually A4) page containing an image of your book cover, with lovely promotional words around them. Waaaay back when I was published with Egmont in the UK, they would send sell sheets with Advance Reader Copies (ARCs) of the book, out to reviewers. They also would have sent these sell sheets out to library suppliers across the UK, because soon after my book came out, I couldn't help googling and *pure joy* there was my book, ready to borrow all over the British Isles.

You need to make one of these sell sheets, which will give librarians who open your email an instant idea of your book and more importantly - your targeted readership.

A sell sheet will need

- A beautiful, high-res image of your book cover
- An enticing blurb indicating the target readership
- A short author bio
- Book measurements and ISBN (ie, paperback, size format, number of pages etc)
- Author contact details should the library invite you to give talks or workshops

Here's one I've prepared earlier.

You can put in a photo of yourself as well, if you like.

Now, that sell sheet is incredibly green and might not be your thing. Here's another that is working very well.

1916-*ish*

"AN ESCAPE STORY THAT WILL KEEP YOU RIVETED TILL THE END."
★★★★★ Dottie, Goodreads

1916-*ish*

EBONY McKENNA

1916-ish - Ebony McKenna
Category: Young Adult
Format: 5x8 paperback 222 pages
ISBN: 978-0-9953839-0-6

Email: author@ebonymckenna.com
Mobile: 0401 484 108

1916-*ish*

History, with a twist.
Time travel, daring adventure and romance await sixteen-year-old exchange student Ingrid Calloway during her visit to France.
When Ingrid joins a war-game re-enactment with local teenagers Luc and Marianne Durand, all hell breaks loose! Gunfire, tanks and explosions become real, as the trio are transported back in time to the perilous trenches of the First World War. It's not a game any more.

As Ingrid struggles to adapt to a dangerous world vastly different to her comfortable 21st century lifestyle, she finds herself attracted to headstrong Luc. But while Ingrid desperately wants to return home, Luc wants to stay put in this quaint pocket of yesteryear. However, these 1916 streets of Paris aren't how observant Ingrid remembers them from her school lessons. Someone is rewriting history.
As events spiral out of control, the teenagers must band together and confront their worst fears, if they're to get back to their own time alive.

About The Author

EBONY MCKENNA is the author of six young adult novels, including the much-loved four-book ONDINE series, which was re-released in paperback in 2017.
Based in Melbourne, Ebony has conducted writing workshops across Australia and is available for school and library visits.
For more 1916-ish information please visit her website:
www.ebonymckenna.com

The cover stands out, but I've also used elements from the cover to make it more dramatic.

Or try using Canva (www.canva.com) to make something pretty.

But what if you don't have the chops to do something like this?

You could ask your cover designer to make a 'sell sheet' for your book.

Or, you could do a search for 'sell sheet templates' and put your book elements in the spaces made by the template (which is what I did for 1916-ish)

Or, you can keep things simple and opt for a plain sheet with clearly set-out information blocks, like the next image:

1. The Summer of Shambles   ISBN 978-0-9953839-1-3   207 pages

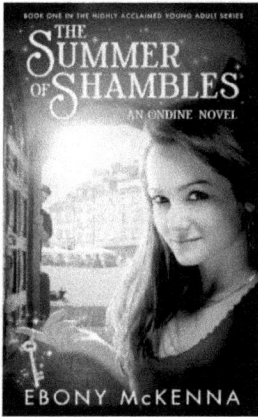

This first book in the ONDINE quartet is filled with adventure, fairytale romance and magical fun. At Psychic Summercamp, fifteen-year-old Ondine doubts she possesses her family's magical abilities. But when her pet ferret Shambles starts talking - in a cheeky Scottish accent no less - anything seems possible. Is Shambles really a young man trapped in a witch's curse, as he claims? And what terrible crime did he commit to deserve such punishment? While Ondine tries to untangle the truth about Shambles, the pair uncover a plot to assassinate a royal family member and unlock the secret to a long-lost treasure. Amongst all this intrigue and mayhem, can Ondine overcome her self-doubts and save the day?

2. The Autumn Palace   ISBN 978-0-9953839-2-0   253 pages

This second sassy adventure in the ONDINE quadrilogy combines fairytale romance with magical fun. Detective duo Ondine and her handsome new boyfriend Hamish - who has a talent for transforming into a ferret - have landed themselves a dangerous mission from The Duke of Brugel. Upon entering the palace grounds they are confronted by a fierce tornado that awakens something dark and ominous. Unexplained phenomena begin intruding on every day life at an alarming rate. Surrounded by strange magic, Ondine and Hamish must expose a royal conspiracy, champion the palace's downtrodden servants and solve a baffling mystery. With so much at stake, will they ever find time for their burgeoning romance to blossom?

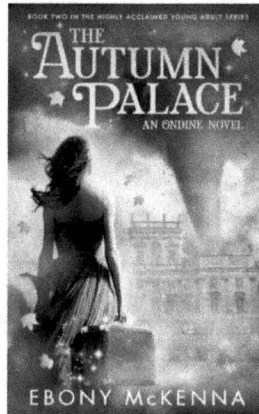

This sell sheet contains most the information a librarian will need - ist has the ISBN, blurb and book dimensions.

What it doesn't have is where to buy the book and how to contact the author. If you put this information in your email, but not on the sell sheet - well, they might get separated and you don't want that.

Your cover here is doing a LOT of work (as it should) because you have a lot of gatekeepers to get through on your book's way to the library shelves.

You need to appeal to library suppliers so they will stock your books.

You need to appeal to librarians so they will buy your books.

You need to appeal to readers who are in an actual library, surrounded by everyone else's books - give them a reason to choose yours over all the others.

A sell sheet is a lot of work and you need to get it right.

EBOOK AUTHORS

You need to make sell sheets as well, so you can show them to libraries across this beautiful country.

Your ebook may be in Overdrive, but the libraries have so many ebooks to choose from, they might not see yours, so send your sell-sheet out to libraries to let them know about your book/s.

An author personally making contact (politely and profession-ally) may sway them towards your title. Or at least remind them you exist.

Keep it fresh, simple, easy to read. Make your cover pop! Woot!

This also means I HAVE TO DO THE HOMEWORK BECAUSE I NEED TO GET MY 'EDIT YOUR OWN' BOOKS OUT THERE AND I HAVE NOT THOUGHT THIS THROUGH AND I might just _{run away.}

CHAPTER 16

CREATING LIBRARY LISTS

NOW WE'RE GOING to create a huge list of all the libraries to contact. You don't have to contact every single one by any means. But it's a handy list - AND next time you're planning a holiday, maybe visit a couple of libraries in the region you're going to. That's always fun.

The focus here will be on contacting public libraries.

SCHOOL LIBRARIES

Young Adult and Middle Grade authors should also make a separate list of all the primary and high schools in your area, so you can contact them and let them know you're a local author, available for school visits etc.

Honestly time:

I have failed spectacularly at this. Sure, I've emailed many high schools on my side of Melbourne, but not one has contacted me directly. Why? Because their funds are so limited. For a start, many primary schools don't have dedicated librarians. But the biggest problem is the school library sticking to its budget. They simply can't buy the books they want to.

School libraries also have speaker agencies contacting them all the time about people available to give school talks.

WORKING WITH CHILDREN CHECK

If you're planning on stepping foot inside a primary or secondary school, get a Working With Children Check. This link takes you to the Victorian site (my home state) so if you're outside Victoria, go to your favourite search engine and type 'working with children check' and add your home state to the search.

How else to be invited into schools?

Pester power from students. When students start bugging their librarians about an amazing author, they're more likely to invite them in. They'll listen to their students more than 'some random author'.

School librarians are, by nature, wonderful people who have a deep and abiding love for books. They visit public libraries all the time.

If your books are in the local public libraries, local students (and school librarians) will see them there and borrow them. Then they'll rave about the books to their friends and hassle their school librarians to get them in. That's the word of mouth magic going on. It can take a very long time for this to happen, by the way.

As a real-life example: Over Christmas 2017, a student (who

used to be at primary school with my dude) told me she'd requested her school get my books in. I thanked her profusely (even though I hadn't received any orders lately.) Then I checked my sales on Blurb and lo, an order had gone through for one of each title in early December.

Consider signing up with a speaker agency, then they do the bookings for you (and set the appearance fees.)

CHECKING ON YOUR BOOKS:

For a quick check of where your books might already be, go to https://trove.nla.gov.au

and search your writing name.

(Ego surfing is the best!)

You never know what will show up in a catalogue somewhere, especially if you've been writing for a few decades.

OK, now you've done that, get ready to make a list of libraries to contact. Libraries that don't have your books. This is a long slog of a job. It's where you create a list of all the public libraries you're going to contact and what order to do it in.

And I'm here to help show you the fastest way to get all those contacts.

TASMANIA

Starting here first, because all public libraries in Tas come under the LINC umbrella, which makes them easy to contact.

Go here and suggest your book title to them and which suppliers they can buy from and LINC will do the rest.

https://libraries.tas.gov.au

Again, check their catalogue to make sure your title isn't already there. Tell them all about your new ones too.

The bonus for contacting LINC in Tas via their online form is you don't need your sell sheets. (Although if you give them your website address, you'll be able to show them your stunning covers.)

VICTORIA

Feast your eyes on this resource:

https://www.localgovernment.vic.gov.au/__data/assets/ pdf_file/0017/512216/2021-Directory-of-Public-Library-Services-in-Victoria.pdf

Regularly updated - this is Feb 2021 - it has every library in the state, along with contact emails and in some cases the name of the librarians or collections managers.

For these libraries, you will need your sell sheets, and plenty of patience as you contact each library individually via email. As much as possible, tailor each email specifically to that council or regional library. Bonus, some shires and local councils have doubled or tripled up, creating a regional library service that covers a dozen libraries across multiple shires. You only need to contact one librarian in each of those regions, not each individual library. The larger library services usually have someone dedicated to your type of book (ie, a youth librarian for younger readers, and a collections manager for general fiction etc.)

SOUTH AUSTRALIA

OK, Click Here and then click on the Locate a Library link.

Scroll down and you'll find links to download the entire list of 130 libraries as a pdf or as a spreadsheet.

WESTERN AUSTRALIA

Many public libraries use the resources from the State Library, so that's a great place to start.

State Library of Western Australia

info@slwa.wa.gov.au

I just checked my name and there are copies of my books are in the State Library's catalogue, which fills me with glee. Even better, all four Ondine's are at a library called Success Public Library. Success? YES!

For the whole state, Click Here and checkout the links, especially the sortable list of public libraries.

NORTHERN TERRITORY

Click here for one link to every public library in the NT.

https://nt.gov.au/leisure/arts-culture-heritage/find-a-library-in-the-nt

QUEENSLAND

This page has a list of every council offering library services. Click Here to get started.

That way you only need to contact the main library, not each branch.

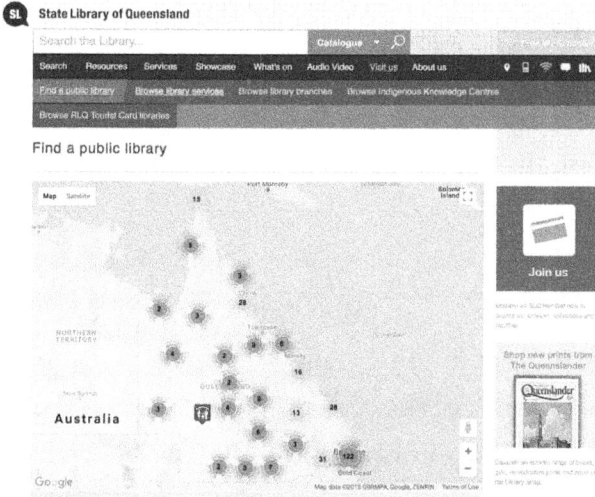

NEW SOUTH WALES

Oh what a treat.

Click here

http://www.sl.nsw.gov.au/public-library-services/about-public-library-services/find-public-library-nsw

and download the Public Library Directory. 105 pages with every public library service, including address and email contacts. Again, this groups each main library service together (which can cover up to a dozen branches) and as a bonus, in many cases the main librarian's name is on the list, so you can personalise your emails to them!

ACT

All libraries in the ACT are part of ACT Government libraries. As such, there's only one email you need to send information to:

library.customerinfo@act.gov.au

I saved the easiest one for last, because I don't know about you, but I'm tired!

NEW ZEALAND

Australians won't get lending rights from our books being in NZ's libraries, but as some of the library suppliers (Like Peter Pal and James Bennett) supply libraries there, it's worth picking up new readers 'across the ditch'.

Go here

http://www.publiclibraries.org.nz/FindALibrary.aspx

With this website, click on the coloured circles, then zoom in to the 'red teardrop' on the map to get the website details of each library. Then get the email address/contact us details from each library.

OMG are you tired? I'm a wreck!

CHAPTER 17

CONTACTING LIBRARIES
CONTACTING LIBRARIES

NOW WE'RE on the home stretch.

Now that you have your enormous list of libraries near and far, it's time to start contacting them.

My tip is start with your local libraries - your closest branches. This is your home base, target them first.

You may even be on first name terms with the local librarians. (Lovely, lovely people!)

Next step, consider all the places across the state (or Australia) where you've lived or worked. Contact them, with your 'local status' claim. For example, I used to work at the Footscray Mail in my journalism days. What joy, the libraries in Maribyrnong stock all the Ondines and *1916-ish*. I told you librarians were lovely!

WHAT'S THE BEST WAY TO CONTACT LIBRARIES?

Individually.

Yep. One at a time. Check out the library service's website and see how many branches they have.

I thought I could be clever and put all my state librarian contacts into an email list and contact them all at the same time.

Guess what?

The email either went straight to junk unopened, or it was opened, but nothing happened. What a screaming disaster! Please learn from my mistake and go back to old fashioned one-at-a-time contacting, where you introduce yourself and your book/s and let them know they can be ordered from all the main suppliers.

SMALL PRESS AUTHORS

Your print or ebooks may already be in some libraries, so you need to know which ones are in their catalogues ahead of time. Why? Because if your earlier books are on the shelves, you'll look a bit unprofessional asking them to buy the same book again.

BUT if your earlier books are in their catalogues, it gives you a talking point for encouraging interest in the next one:

"I'm delighted my titles 'THE BEST BOOK EVER' and its sequel 'THE EVEN BETTEREST BOOK' are in your library catalogue. Now the trequel is here, 'THE EVEN BETEREST BOOKEST.'

Then let them know which suppliers stock your book, and cross your fingers that they order more in.

If the library has all your books already, then give yourself a pat on the back for writing a brilliant book that people want to read. Then move on to contacting the next library.

I'd be reluctant to put 'my books are already in 'next shire along's catalogue' in an email, in an attempt to show them you're already successful. Libraries have strict budgets, but they don't restrict borrowing privileges to people in their immediate local government area. If you specifically mention to the City of Yarra that your books are in Port Philip's libraries, (as an example) they might shrug and say, 'we'll tell our borrowers to borrow from them, if they ask for your book.' Many libraries are pooling their resources and sharing shelf space to make their budgets stretch further.

True story, my neighbour has recently acquired an ereader and he's signed up for four library services across Eastern Melbourne. He's utterly delighted because he doesn't have to drive to those libraries to borrow - just put in a request and when the book is available, it pops up on his device.

As I said in the previous chapter, my books are in some libraries across WA, but I've never approached any of them independently. The reason they're on the shelves is because the library suppliers did the work for me and promoted my books (along with thousands of others).

DON'T DONATE YOUR BOOKS

This absolutely bears repeating.

Aside from sounding like a nice idea, please don't donate your books to your local library - unless you know they really want them.

Put it another way: If you were making clothes and all your friends loved them and said you should make more and sell them, would you take a carload to Myer and say, 'Put these on the racks?'

It's the same with books.

I've spoken to authors who have donated their books and the results aren't that good. One said she donated a paperback to her closest library and a year later found it out in the second hand sale. Books that don't get borrowed don't stay on the shelves for long. And, if the book was donated, it might not even be put on the shelf in the first place.

Yes, I'm repeating myself because this is so important. Plus, you've bought a guide book on how to do it the right way, so why buy the proverbial dog if you're going to bark yourself?

I also know, having grown up with a stack of teachers and librarians in my life, that they have an ordered way of doing things. Libraries have long standing collections policies, setting out how they order books and which shelving areas need replenishing and which are overstocked. Publishers send out advance promotions about upcoming titles months in advance - so libraries can allocate their budgets.

Doing things the right way around will help the author and the library in the long run.

PART THREE CHECKLIST

- You've made sell sheets.
- You've made a list of libraries to contact
- You're drafting emails ready to send (or being really brave and already sending them! Huzzah!)

- You're collapsing in a heap because this is so much work!

Time for a cup of tea (or something stronger) and a lie down.

CHAPTER 18

BRINGING IT ALL TOGETHER

IS THERE anything I've missed? Anything you don't have a handle on? Please email me author@ebonymckenna.com and I'll add it to the next edition. The joy of ebooks is they are a living document that I can update - and everyone who's already bought it will receive those updates as new information comes to hand.

Contacting libraries was the last thing to do on the jobs list, and yet it was probably the first thing you *wanted* to do. Now that you know how 'the system' works, it will be much easier getting your next book (and the one after that) into the system, so the system starts to work for you.

Over the last year, I've come across some fabulous, helpful people, and they've been wonderful. Others were trying to be helpful, but weren't really able to help that much. It's the nature of the industry that you'll have hits and misses.

You really can't please everyone.

CHAPTER 19

SCHOOL SUPPLIERS

WITH REGARDS TO SCHOOL LIBRARIES, most will be looking to stock children's and young adult fiction. Or 'Lichery' books. If your books fit in those categories, it might be worth contacting the following:

SCHOLASTIC AND OTHER TYPES OF BOOK CLUBS

These book club newsletters go out across the country, into schools (usually primary schools.) Kids (well, their parents) order discounted books, the school also gets a few books for their library and everyone is happy.

Personally, I don't see this as a guaranteed way of getting into school libraries, but every little helps, right?

My first book has appeared in these book clubs, either solo or bundled in with other similar books. Your publisher doesn't have to be Scholastic to get in, by the way (mine was Hardie Grant

Egmont at the time.) But since I've gone indie, I haven't even approached them. Perhaps I should?

It's possible, if you're writing for younger readers, to get an independent book in their book club, but you'd probably have to offer it at an incredible discount. I'm not sure you'd make much of a profit, but on the other hand it could be an excellent way to reach plenty of readers.

REDGUM BOOK CLUB

NSW-based, Redgum Book Club goes out to schools offering new and discounted books and book sets, similar to Scholastic. It's well worth a google search and checking them out. They have supported indie authors in the past and I hear good things about them.

LAMONT BOOKS IN HALLAM, VICTORIA

Lamont sells directly into primary and secondary schools in Australia (mostly Victoria). They like a good 'lead time' of at least three months for a new title, in order to decide whether to stock it.

Last year I offered them *Robyn and the Hoodettes* but they turned it down because it was already released. (And there I was thinking it was new!)

But then I told them about my next book, *The Girl and The Ghost* and they were interested. They asked to read it first (yikes, I felt like I was back on submission!)

They read it.

Exactly! Lamont staff read all the books they sell, so that when they recommend books to schools, they know what they're talking about. In the end, they got back to me and said, 'yes thanks' and they placed an order for 50 books. I was pretty happy with that.

I now know how early I need to contact them for the next book, which is excellent. I love them like whoa!

The downside is they want a very deep discount on the $RRP. 65-70% usually.

ASO- AUSTRALIAN STANDING ORDERS

I contacted Belinda Bolliger from ASO - Australian Standing Orders. They supply schools with books for reading lists or for the library shelves, but a fairly narrow range of titles.

"ASO buys books from established publishers as well as self-publishers/independent authors. We buy for all age groups, from preschool through to secondary. We select titles that can generally be described as the 'literary' end of children's publishing (ie, not mass market or strongly commercial titles), the style of book that is likely to end up on the CBCA shortlist, for example.

We only buy first release titles and send them to schools in the month of their publication. We do not take backlist titles.

Quantities for young adult titles are around 900 copies. Quantities for junior fiction titles around 2,000 copies.

We buy at either 65% discount/25% returns or 70% firm sale, depending on the deal, quantities required etc.

I need to read complete, edited manuscripts approximately 4 months ahead of publication. I am currently finalising June selections and will begin on July selections next month.

Please note that there is only one of me, so it's best to send a sales information sheet before sending a manuscript for consideration. I can then let you know if I'm interested in reading the manuscript.

I'm happy to receive manuscripts by email, however if the files are very large, I suggest that you send them via Wetransfer or Dropbox, or something similar.

Belinda Bolliger

Editorial Manager, **Australian Standing Orders**

Scholastic Australia Pty Ltd | PO Box 579 Lindfield, NSW, 2070 | 345 Pacific Highway, Lindfield, NSW, 2070

(02) 9413 8342

belinda_bolliger@australianstandingorders.com.au

THE LITTLE BOOKROOM, CARLTON, VICTORIA

Leesa Lambert is the owner operator and she knows and loves books. I love going there to buy books - especially for fussy boys. (I bristle at the term 'reluctant reader'. My son will read the local newspaper, but finds a slab of small-print text really daunting. He's not reluctant, he just loves pictures in his books.) I digress.

The Little Bookroom sells to the public from their shopfront, and they sell books directly to schools via their sales reps. I have them to thank for the vast amount of the first two Ondines ending up in so many school libraries.

I'm in Victoria, and Lamont and The Little Bookroom are here in Melbourne, so it makes sense that I've contacted 'local' suppliers.

GOOGLE IS YOUR FRIEND

It's worth spending some time googling library book suppliers in your state to see what comes up closer to you. Most of them will be companies that supply chairs, tables, shelves, trolleys, stickers and labels. Everything but the books. But some actually sell books!

This link is from the PLA, Public Libraries of Australia. It's a full list of stacks of library suppliers - but not all of them supply books. However, it's a brilliant resource, so I'm sharing it here.

http://www.pla.org.au/Library_Suppliers?
field_supplier_state_value=All&page=0

CHAPTER 20

ONE MORE THING

PLEASE GO TO MY WEBSITE, www.ebonymckenna.com and join my reader community.

By doing so, you'll get a free young adult ghost story.

I also write regency romances and am having a ball! So if you join my reader community, you'll get the heads-up on free and discounted books, and other great exclusives.

Also, I've caught the formatting bug and can format your manuscripts into ebooks and print books. So basically I have books about editing, run a formatting service and now have this handy guide for getting your books into libraries so you can sell more books and earn royalties. I'm like a midwife for books to get out there into the world!

I have loved creating this workshop/guidebook. The feedback I've had so far has been brilliant. Authors are sharing their successes with me and I couldn't be happier.

I hope you're feeling confident and filled with knowledge (so much knowledge) to get your books out there on to library shelves.

Thank you so much for being awesome!
Much love,
Ebony

PART 4

TROUBLESHOOTING

CHAPTER 21

MARC RECORDS

I'M GIVING subject a chapter on its own so you can find it easily. Hey, there *waves*.

This is in response to the feedback I've received since first publishing this book - and all the feedback has been about MARC records not working out properly when authors register to earn back some of those beautiful Lending Rights.

What is a MARC record?

MARC stands for **MA**chine **R**eadable **C**ataloguing record.

If you fill in your book's details on myidentifiers.com.au (as we all need to) and then go and fill all your details into your printer/distributor such as Ingram Spark - those details need to be **exactly the same.**

I'm talking EXACT!

If you have different keywords, or a slightly different description, or different page numbers - the MARC record will not match up and you won't be able to register for Lending Rights.

It won't matter if you've sent copies off to the National Library or not (as some helpful folks at the Lending Rights department suggest).

In the 'Registering for Lending Rights' chapter in Part II, I explained it like this:

> **"Match Your Categories**
>
> Not only will you need to make sure the ISBN is spot on, and your titles are correctly matched; you'll need to make sure your book description is the same. Otherwise Lending Rights will have a fit and you'll get 'computer says no' treatment. Maintain consistency with correct titles, description, ISBN, publisher, keywords/categories. If there's a mismatch, Lending Rights will query your 'MARC'. MARC stands for **Ma**chine **R**eadable **C**ataloguing record, and you can burn your noggin reading about it here."

It's an easy thing to miss, which is why I'm making this chapter, so that it stands out.

It is also easy to accidentally put the wrong information in to online forms, so I urge everyone to keep good records.

To recap:

You will need to buy ISBNs for print editions in order to list them for Lending Rights in Australia.

To buy ISBNs in Australia you need to purchase them through the registered retailer, Thorpe Bowker and use their myidentifiers.com.au website to list all the details of that book with the ISBN.

Keep a record of everything you've put in myidentifiers (copy and paste into a word file if you need to) so that when you come to list your book and its ISBN and details with your printer (and with Lending Rights), you're copying and pasting the exact same information from one place to the other.

If you get rejected from Lending Rights because of the MARC record issue, then you'll need to go back through your own records and rejig them. Copy and paste everything from myidentifyers into a word document. Or take screen shots. Which ever way is easier for you to 'spot the difference'.

If there's something in myidentifiers that you can't change (perhaps it's an imprint that's come up under your real name rather than your author name) then contact myidentifiers and ask them for assistance.

Do the same for your printer/distributor (such as Blurb. com.au or Ingram Spark or Amazon etc)

Make sure every section you fill out matches the information on the other forms. Double check against the ISBN, page count, title, spelling, keywords, etc etc. Make sure everything is as exact as possible.

If there's a space that doesn't require filling (an optional field) leave it blank so there's one less thing to go wrong.

Drink all the coffee/tea/gin.

When you're absolutely certain the details in myidentifiers and your printer are exact, take those details and enter them into your Lending Rights claim and make sure they're exactly the same as well.

I have self-published 7 novels and 3 writing guides, and only one novel has come back with the 'MARC' situation. So I know that 9 out of 10 submissions I've made to Lending Rights have gone through. It's up to me to go back and fix that novel (which, y'know, human nature and all ... can I really be bothered? Yes, yes I should.)

Good luck with it all.

More coffee.

Love Ebs

ABOUT THE AUTHOR

NON-FICTION AUTHOR GUIDES

Edit Your Own Romance Novel
Marketing Your Book To Australian Libraries
The Ticking Clock
Author Emails
Author Business College

YOUNG ADULT FICTION

The Ondine Series:
The Summer of Shambles
The Autumn Palace
The Winter of Magic
The Spring Revolution
A Brugel Fairytale Treasury

Stand-alone novels:
1916-ish
Robyn and the Hoodettes

The Girl and The Ghost - RWA 2018 Romantic Book of the Year winner.

Outback Yankee

Writing Regency Romance as Ebony Oaten

Unsuitable Suitors:

Marquess and Tell

Me and Mr Jones

Weekend at Baron E's

There's Something About Miss Mary

Fetch The Earl - coming December 2021

Miss Remington's Steely Resolve - coming December 2021

Writing Contemporary Romance as Ebony Jean

Cupid Games

Ripe for the Picking

Click here to join Ebony's Reading Community. Be first to hear about new releases, discount offers, free reads, cat photographs and the occasional 'bake fail'.

www.ebonymckenna.com

Come and waste some time with me on social media

facebook.com/EbonyMcKenna

twitter.com/WriterEbony

ACKNOWLEDGMENTS

Enormous thanks to the Romance Writers of Australia for being an incredible support network, and to the authors who signed up for this workshop, to road-test it and prove it works. You are awesome.

To my wonderful crit group, The Saturday Ladies' Bridge Club. We rock!